ROTHERHAM LIBRARY & INFORMATION SERVICE

CCS

Sources of Light

Louise and Richard
Spilsbury

raintree

a Capstone company — publishers for children

Raintree is an imprint of Capstone Global Library Limited, a company incorporated in England and Wales having its registered office at 7 Pilgrim Street, London, EC4V 6LB – Registered company number: 6695582

www.raintree.co.uk
myorders@raintree.co.uk

Text © Capstone Global Library Limited 2016
The moral rights of the proprietor have been asserted.

Edited by Penny West
Designed by Rich Parker
Picture research by Tracy Cummins
Production by Helen McCreath
Originated by Capstone Global Library Ltd
Printed and bound in China by CTPS

ISBN 978 1 406 29911 3
19 18 17 16 15
10 9 8 7 6 5 4 3 2 1

Spilsbury, Louise and Richard
Sources of Light (Exploring Light)

British Library Cataloguing in Publication Data
A full catalogue record for this book is available from the British Library.

Acknowledgements
We would like to thank the following for permission to reproduce photographs:
Capstone Press: HL Studios, 22, Karon Dubke, 7, 8, 9, 12, 13, 16, 17, 20, 21, 24, 25, 28, 29; Getty Images: Karen Doody/ Stocktrek Image, 23; Shutterstock: agsandrew, Design Element, Click Bestsellers, Design Element, Dennis Tokarzewski, Design Element, Dmitry Bruskov, 18, dwph, 5, focal point, 27, ID1974, Design Element, luckypic, Design Element, Maridav, 19, noppharat, 4, PandaWild, 15, Tom Reichner, 10, Valentyn Volkov, 14, Vass Zoltan, Design Element, wavebreakmedia, 11, welcomia, 6; Thinkstock: Anatoly Vartanov, 26.

Cover photo of Rudimental performing at Exit Festival in Novi Sad, Serbia reproduced with permission of Shutterstock/ Jelena Ivanovic.

We would like to thank Catherine Jones for her invaluable help in the preparation of this book.

Every effort has been made to contact copyright holders of material reproduced in this book. Any omissions will be rectified in subsequent printings if notice is given to the publisher.

All the Internet addresses (URLs) given in this book were valid at the time of going to press. However, due to the dynamic nature of the Internet, some addresses may have changed, or sites may have changed or ceased to exist since publication. While the author and publisher regret any inconvenience this may cause readers, no responsibility for any such changes can be accepted by either the author or the publisher.

Contents

Some words are shown in bold, **like this**. You can find out what they mean by looking in the glossary.

Sources of light

Light is something we use every day without thinking. We just flick on a light switch or turn on the computer and there it is. A **source** of light is something that makes or gives off light. A lamp is a source of light. The book the lamp shines on is not. Sources of light are very important. They allow us to see the world around us. Imagine what the world would be like without sources of light!

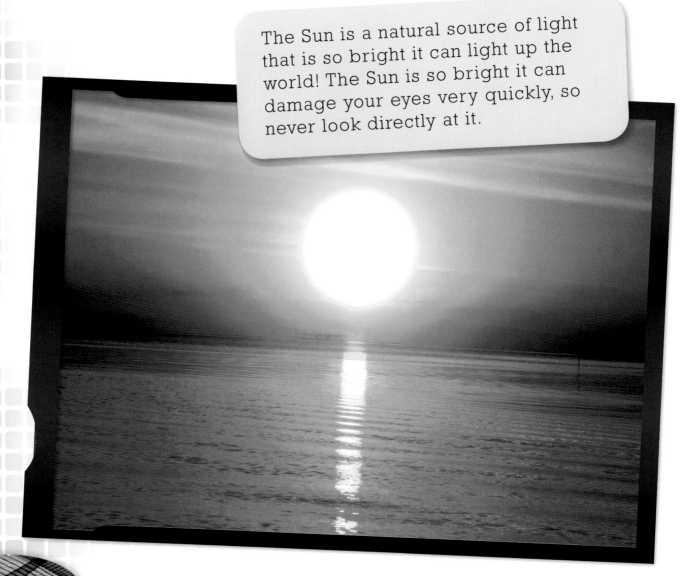

The Sun is a natural source of light that is so bright it can light up the world! The Sun is so bright it can damage your eyes very quickly, so never look directly at it.

Fireworks that light up the night sky are created by people.

A flash of lightning, the Sun and the other stars are natural sources of light. Light sources made by people include torches, computers and lamps. They use batteries and **electricity** to work. Which light sources are you using to read this book?

Be a light detective

Investigate the light sources around you. Take a walk around your school or home and write down as many sources of light as you can. You might be surprised how many you find!

Light on the move

Light is useful to us because it can travel away from its **source**. Sunlight moves through space and lights up Earth. Light spreads out from a torch and shows our path. Light can move because it is a form of **energy**. Energy is the power that makes things work or move. Light energy travels in straight lines called **rays**. You can see this when you look at the beam of a torch.

We can see light travelling in straight lines in the powerful beams made by a lighthouse.

Round light bulbs allow light rays to leave them and spread out in all directions. This maximises the light they produce.

A torch shines light in one direction only, so it is easy to see that light travels in straight lines. Light from a round light bulb can spread in all directions. The light rays travel in straight lines in different directions. That is why a light on a ceiling can light up a whole room.

Less light!

As light gets further away from a light source, it spreads out more. As light spreads out more, it looks less bright. That is because the light is spread over a wider area. Also, that is why the further you get from a light source, the less bright it looks.

Activity: The speed of light

Light and sound are both forms of **energy** and they can both move. Try this activity to find out if light travels faster than sound.

What you need

- four balloons
- two friends to help
- a pin.

What to do

1 Inflate the four balloons and tie the ends.

2 Ask your friends to stand in one place while you walk about 4 metres (13 feet) away from them with the balloons. Stop and pop one balloon.

3 Your friends should all write down which came first: seeing the balloon pop or hearing the sound of the pop. They should not talk to each other about their answers.

4 Walk so you're a further 4 metres (13 feet) away and pop a balloon again. Do this twice more until you have popped all the balloons.

5 What did your friends notice?

What happens?

Your friends should see the balloons pop slightly before they hear the balloons pop. This is easier to spot the further away from the balloon they are. This proves that light energy can move faster than sound energy through air. Light is nearly a million times faster than sound. In one second, light could travel seven and a half times around the world!

Is it a light source?

Light **sources** make their own light, so we can see them even when it is completely dark. That is why torches are so useful at night! Objects that do not make their own light are not light sources. We can only see them when **rays** of light from a light source **reflect**, or bounce, off their surface. When light hits an object, some is reflected and enters our eyes. That is how we see the object.

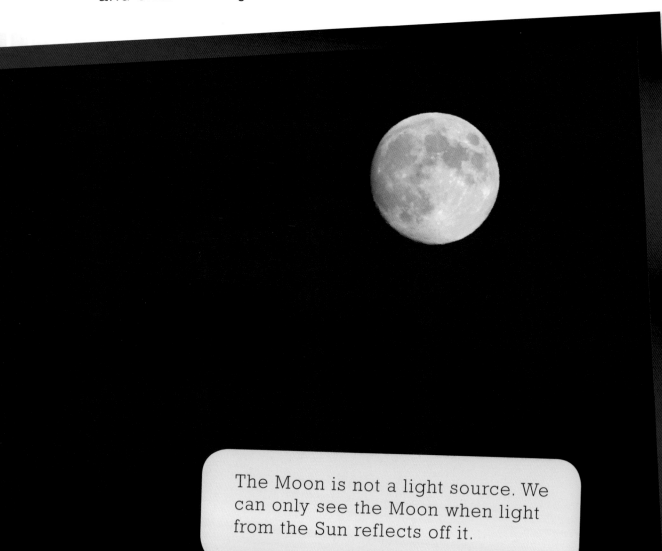

The Moon is not a light source. We can only see the Moon when light from the Sun reflects off it.

Shiny objects like this disco ball are not light sources, but they reflect light very well.

Mirrors and other objects reflect light so well it can look as if they are sources of light, too. That is why they look shiny. But they can only shine when light from a light source reflects off them. A shiny object will not shine in darkness.

Reflecting light

When many rays of light hit an object, they bounce off in different directions. When reflected rays hit our eyes, we see the object they are reflecting off. In a brightly lit room, it feels as if light is all around us because the walls reflect light from a light source in all directions.

Activity: Shine a light

Test what happens to light **sources** with distance and less **energy**.

What to do

1 Tape the sheet of graph paper low down on a wall, not far above the floor.

2 Stack the books so that when you lay the torch on them, the torch is level with the graph paper.

What you need

- sticky tape
- a sheet of graph paper
- big books
- a small torch with new batteries inside
- a metre rule or tape measure
- paper and pencil.

3 Measure 1 metre (3 feet) away from the wall and put the stack of books and torch here. Turn off the lights in the room and turn on the torch so it shines on the centre of the graph paper. Measure or count the number of squares that are lit up by the torch. Write down the number.

4 Measure and move the books and torch 1.5 metres (4 feet), 2 metres (6 feet), 2.5 metres (8 feet) and 3 metres (9 feet) away from the wall, or further if you like. Repeat the test and count the squares the torch lights up each time. What do you notice?

5 Leave the torch on for about an hour (or until your torch light looks weaker) and then do the same tests again. Repeat every hour until the torch batteries run out.

What happens?

When the torch is moved further away from the wall, it covers a bigger area of the graph paper. The light spreads out. As it spreads out, it gets dimmer. The torch batteries use energy to make the torch work. As the batteries run out of energy, the torch gives out less light.

Heat and light

Many light **sources** make light because they are hot. When we strike a match, **chemicals** at the tip catch fire. The wood of the match burns and some of its heat **energy** changes into light energy. Blowing the match puts out the light but it may still produce enough heat energy to burn. That is why we need to be careful when using matches, candles and other flames as light sources.

Different types of energy can be changed from one form to another. Chemical energy in wood turns to heat and light energy when it burns.

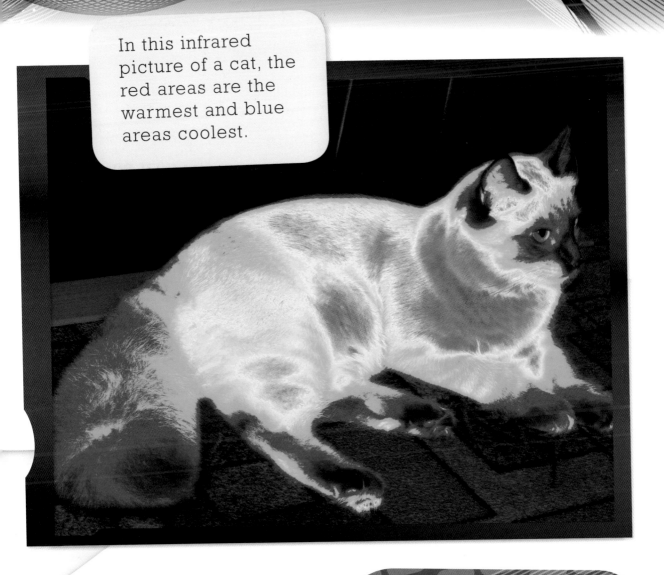

In this infrared picture of a cat, the red areas are the warmest and blue areas coolest.

The melted rock or lava oozing from a volcano is not on fire but is much hotter than matches. The heat energy is so high that it makes the lava glow red. Much, much hotter objects, such as the Sun, glow white and very bright because they release even more light energy.

Invisible light!

Animals produce heat energy. It travels in **rays** like light energy. We cannot see it because our eyes cannot detect it.

Activity: Hot light

Light **sources** often make heat. Test this out using desk lamps and thermometers.

What to do

1 Position each desk lamp over a sheet of white paper, with a distance of about 10 centimetres (4 inches) between the bulb and the paper.

2 Place a thermometer directly beneath each bulb, on the paper.

What you need

- two desk lamps: one fitted with an **incandescent** bulb, the other fitted with a **fluorescent** bulb. The bulbs should be of equivalent brightness.
- two sheets of white paper
- two digital thermometers
- an adult to help.

3 Switch the lamps on. After 5 minutes, record the temperature under each lamp using the thermometer.

Try this!

Solar collectors are devices people put on roofs. They have **liquid** inside that warms up easily in sunlight. The liquid is used to help heat water for people to use. Try making your own solar collectors by filling and sealing water bottles and leaving them outside on sunny days!

What happens?

You should find that one bulb produces a higher temperature than the other. This is because different types of lamp produce different amounts of heat **energy** as they produce light. We say that fluorescent lamps are energy efficient because they do not waste as much energy as heat when making light.

17

The Sun

Our planet's most important **source** of light is the Sun. The Sun is a gigantic ball of glowing **gas**, like all stars in the universe. Stars glow brightly and produce temperatures that are hundreds of thousands of times hotter than the hottest oven. Some of this enormous amount of **energy** travels to Earth as the **rays** of light and heat we know as sunlight.

The Sun is our closest star. It lights up and warms Earth, even when it is partly hidden behind the clouds.

Sunlight's warmth helps fruit and vegetables to ripen so they are good to eat.

Sunlight is vital for plants to grow and make their own food. Many animals survive by eating plants and other animals eat the plant eaters. People even turn sunlight into **electricity** using devices called **solar panels**!

A long way away

Sunlight lights and warms us even though the Sun is millions of kilometres from Earth. Light moves at 300,000 kilometres (186,412 miles) per second but it still takes 8 minutes to reach us from the Sun! But that is much closer than our next nearest star. Its light takes over 4 years to reach us.

Activity: Sunny beans

This activity shows how plants need sunlight to grow.

What to do

1 Fold up two sheets of kitchen roll, moisten and place in one jar. Repeat for the second jar.

2 Put one bean down the side of the jar, so it is between the kitchen roll and the glass (so you can see it from the side of the jar).

What you need

- four sheets kitchen roll
- a sprayer filled with water
- two glass jars with lids
- two bean seeds
- aluminium foil.

3 Put the lids on the jars and wrap one completely in foil so the inside of it is dark.

bean grown
in the light

bean grown
in the dark

4 Leave both jars on a light, warm windowsill for 10 days, opening each to spray the seeds with water every few days.

Try this

Once the seedling has emerged from the seed, place its jar at one end of a shoe box sealed shut. Carefully cut a small hole in the lid at the opposite end. Did your plant grow towards the light?

What happens?

Both seeds **germinate**, or grow, proving that sunlight is not needed for this first stage in a plant's life. But the main shoot of the plant kept in the dark is less green and more spindly. Its leaves are withered and pale. Light is needed for the young plant to grow the green leaves it can use to make food and thrive.

Cool lights

Not all light **sources** get hot to give off light. When you crack a glowstick, tubes inside containing different **chemicals** break so they start to mix together. This produces a chemical change that releases some **energy** as light and very little as heat energy. The stick stops glowing once all the chemicals are mixed and used up.

We can see objects such as some watch faces in the dark at night or under the bed covers because energy from light is continuing to make special chemicals glow.

Caribbean reef squid can change their colour patterns to communicate with other squid. They are even able to create one pattern on their left side to send one message, and a different one on their right!

Some animals can give off light in a similar way to glowsticks. Male fireflies use patterns of light flashes to tell female fireflies where they are. They take in air and mix it with a substance inside their body to make a light with almost no heat at all.

Light to catch prey

Female anglerfish have a rod above their mouth tipped with a light source. Shrimp and other small creatures are attracted to the light and the anglerfish gulps them up when they get close enough!

Activity: Light from sugar

Some **materials** become light **sources** when they are crushed, torn or rubbed. One of these is a common, sweet kitchen ingredient.

Warning!
Do this with an adult and be gentle so you do not break the glass or the plate.

What you need
- white sugar cubes
- a plate
- a flat-bottomed and strong drinking glass.

What to do

1 Place a sugar cube on the plate.

2 Push firmly but gently down on the sugar cubes, rocking the glass. Do not bang the glass on the plate. Repeat several times so you get used to crushing the sugar cubes carefully. You can leave all the crushed sugar on the plate.

Try this

Some sticky substances can also become light sources when ripped in the dark!

- Seal and then rip open a self-sealable envelope
- Fold a length of duct tape in half so it is stuck to itself leaving each end folded over by 1 cm (half an inch). Then rip apart!

3 Now crush new sugar cubes using this method in a very dark room with all the lights turned off. What do you see?

What happens?

You should see flashes of glowing blue light from the crushed sugar cubes because some **energy** from crushing the sugar changes into light energy. This light is so weak that it can only be seen faintly in a very dark room and not in a lit room.

Using light sources

People have made special light **sources** to use in different ways. **Lasers** are machines that make narrow, powerful beams of light. The beams can be used to play DVDs and for cutting things accurately and carefully. In factories, lasers cut through tough metals or hundreds of layers of fabric at once!

Laser beams do not spread out like ordinary light. They can be focused in one direction to do a job.

Bar codes

Bar codes are the strips of lines you see on shop labels. A bar code reader uses a laser beam to scan bar codes. It detects the line widths and spacing on the bar code to identify the item and its price.

A bundle of optical fibres as thin as a little finger can carry tens of thousands of light messages at once. That is far more information than a normal cable the thickness of your arm could carry!

People also use light sources to send information. For example, phone messages can be changed into patterns of light flashes and sent through very long **optical fibres**. Optical fibres are thin, flexible and transparent glass rods. The light flashes move through the rods without shining out from the sides.

Activity: Pouring light

Try sending a light message without **optical fibres**, using a bottle of water and a torch!

What you need

- a clear plastic bottle, such as a medium fizzy drink bottle
- aluminium foil
- sticky tape
- a dark room with a sink, such as a bathroom
- a torch.

What to do

1 Wrap the bottle completely in foil, but leave the base bare. Use sticky tape to secure the foil.

2 Fill the bottle almost to the top with water. Then switch on your torch and turn off the lights.

3 Shine the torch through the bare base of the bottle as you hold the bottle on its side and start to gently and slowly pour the water into a sink. Hold the bottle as high as you can without splashing water on the floor! Keep the torch close to the base of the bottle at all times.

What happens?

Hopefully you will see a spot of bright light where the water hits the sink. This is because almost all of the light from the torch is **reflected** every time it hits the edge of the stream of water. Therefore the light moves from the **source** along the path of the water as it pours.

Glossary

chemical distinct or particular substance that is the same all the way through. Some chemicals are natural, such as water. Other chemicals are made by people, such as the chlorine used in swimming pools.

electricity type of energy we usually use to make machines work

energy the power that makes things work or move

fluorescent something that makes light when electricity flows through a tube filled with a type of gas

gas thing that has no shape or size of its own. Gases, such as the air around us, can spread out in all directions and change shape to fit any space.

germinate to start to grow. Plant seeds germinate.

incandescent giving out light energy because it is heated

laser narrow, very powerful beam of light used in DVDs, CDs and to cut through things

liquid thing that is runny and cannot be held easily in your hands, such as water, milk or juice

material something we use or make other things from, such as wood, rubber or plastic

optical fibre thin rod of high-quality glass that carries messages coded in light signals

ray narrow line or beam of light

reflect to bounce back off a surface

solar panel panel that absorbs the Sun's rays and uses their energy to make electricity or heat

source person or thing that starts something. A light source gives off light.

Find out more

Books

Flash! Light and How We See Things (The Real Scientist), Peter Riley (Franklin Watts, 2012)

Light (Project Science), Sally Hewitt (Franklin Watts, 2013)

Light and Sound (Mind Webs), Anna Claybourne (Wayland, 2014)

The Sun (Fact Cat), Alice Harman (Wayland, 2014)

Websites

www.bbc.co.uk/bitesize/ks2/science/physical_processes/light/read/1/
On this BBC website you can read more about sources of light.

www.cbv.ns.ca/sydmines/modules/mastop_publish/files/ files_4dd3be55b85bc.pdf
This PDF has lots of examples of light sources.

kidshealth.org/kid/watch/out/summer_safety.html
This website includes important information about how to be safe in the Sun.

optics.synopsys.com/learn/kids/optics-kids-about-lasers.html
On this website you can find out more about lasers and light.

Index